•Don't Quote Me

The Quote Book

copyright©2019

•Don't Quote Me

Written by **Dwayne A. Cannon**

(Inspired By Life)

copyright©2020

•Don't Quote Me

Publisher: **Emerge Productions Group LLC.**

Front Cover Illustration by: **Alamy.com / Emerge Pro Group**

Back Cover Illustration by: **Emerge Pro Group**

- **Don't Quote Me**

(Informal Acronym)

TRU•TH /trooTH/ noun

•*The Real Undeniably Told Honestly*

•Don't Quote Me

(Salutation)

I am filled with excitement and enthusiasm and it is also a pleasure, to have the opportunity to thank everyone who purchased this book and was a part of its inspiration. Thank-you all for being part of my genuine inventiveness that wholeheartily and personally inspired me to write this arrangement and collection of unique, innovative and original quotes.

I also would like to thank everyone, who uses blasphemy to disrespect good writers' energy, those who verbally continue implanting in the world, their incredible animosity and passionate hate. Because without you all, there wouldn't be any Positivity, Prosperity or Peace.

Salute…

•Don't Quote Me

(Synopsis)

This Original, Innovative, Thoughtful and Inspirational quote book entitled "Don't Quote Me" Has put into perspective all original quotes, with a creative point of view intending to inspire its readers. This book is incomparable, with structure that gives you an informative visual. "Don't Quote Me" will not disappoint you and if you're into originality, then this book is definitely for you. You will appreciate the sharp wit, clever observation and resourceful text that incites the imagination, not only does it make you think, but at the same time it will definitely make you want to Quote Me!

- **Don't Quote Me**

(The Quote Book)

A *written arrangement and collection of unique, innovative and original quotes...*

- **QUOTATION SUNDAY**

•Don't Quote Me

(Quotes)

Don't be fooled by fools

Spell Greatness with your name

You can stop and think, at the same time

•Don't Quote Me

*F*ight with your fist, box with your mind

*T*ake all the time out you need
•To know exactly what time it is

*I*f you want people to respect you
•Do something that's very respectful

•Don't Quote Me

*E*verything falls right in place

•When your higher power, drops it in front of you

*M*ake sense to the youth

•By changing their way of thinking

*L*isten to the people who pay more attention

•When listening to you

•Don't Quote Me

*S*urviving is more than just staying alive
•It's a long-term way of living

*D*on't get asked a question
•Then answer the same question, with a question

*A*ny frame of success, will create a beautiful picture
•But any picture in a struggling frame
will forever be unattractive

•Don't Quote Me

Use your time wisely

•By never wasting, a wise person's time

Stay away from people who used to talk to you

•Now all of a sudden, they're quiet, whenever your around

You can cut through all the stress in your life

•By simply sharpening up your life

•Don't Quote Me

*N*ever let a sick minded person
•Prevent you from thinking well

•PASSAGE

MONDAY

•Don't Quote Me

*M*inds that are judgmental

•Should be thinking in court

*G*reat minds don't just think ' alike

•They like to think

*S*ome people wake up, from the ignorance of other people

•Just to go back to sleep

•Don't Quote Me

*K*eeping both of your eyes on the prize

•Will give you a better view of the gift

*Y*ou can always tell if a person is lying

•By simply telling them a lie

*M*ake sure you stop and look both ways

•Before crossing your enemies in the street

•Don't Quote Me

People who live their life, telling a bunch of lies

• Will eventually die withholding, a whole lot of truth

Heaven is what you make it

•And Hell, is what we all will eventually go through

Your first instinct is based on

•When your second thought, is just a little bit skeptical

•Don't Quote Me

Why be around a class of people, who hate their enemies
•When you're still getting schooled,
on how to love your own friends

Sometimes you have to bite your tongue
•In order to get people to feel, what you are saying

Judging a person by their cover
• Makes you the Lawyer, Prosecutor and the Jury

•Don't Quote Me

Wake up, when chasing the appetite in your dreams

• Or continue going to bed hungry, from not feeding your goals

A closed mouth doesn't get fed

•But an open mind, will always remember how to eat

When your hunger for peace kicks in

•Remember, you'll need a heart in order to feed it

•EXCERPT

TUESDAY

•Don't Quote Me

*A*lways strive to create a better future, that's out of this world
•Something, that will make aliens smile

*T*ired of sleeping on the way you should be thinking
•Then wake up, get out of bed, and make up your mind

*T*ry patting a person on the back
•And congratulating them, without using a knife

•Don't Quote Me

If you're constantly walking on somebody's heels
•*Then you should try on their shoes*

Tell people the truth, before you start believing the lies
•*People have been going around telling about you*

Write to exercise your creative thoughts
•*And always remember, the importance of your imagination*

•Don't Quote Me

If God, directs your whole-hearted intentions
•*How can the Devil, interfere with how you're thinking*

Drive your inspiration on a road that's right
•*So, you won't crash when your motivation makes a left turn*

Be the Parent who's not still growing up
•*Trying to figure out how to raise a child*

•Don't Quote Me

When you've already won the situation
•Remember, the outcome doesn't even matter

Some people you should just leave alone already
•Especially if you were already alone, once they decided to leave

Why continue letting people sell you million-dollar dreams
•When every day, you wake up to poor nightmares for free

•RECITE

WEDNESDAY

•Don't Quote Me

Never let what you haven't accomplished
   •Prevent you from getting inspired
   by other people's accomplishments

When the lies people tell gets you intoxicated
•And the truth you know they're concealing, sobers you up
   •Stop drinking with them

Never feel discourage, because you're not every bodies cup of tea
   • Because personally, I don't know too many tea drinkers
   • Who didn't at least once in their life, ask for a cup of coffee

•Don't Quote Me

Even if you chop the right hand off, a person who steals
- *What's stopping them from raising their left hand*
  - *And swearing to God they're not a thief*

Once you divorce a negative thought
- *And start a whole new relationship, with a positive idea*
- *You'll never again feel guilty, about cheating on your mind*

Some people love taking kindness for weakness
- *Until they meet that one person,' who's weakness*
  - *Is all about not loving their kind*

•Don't Quote Me

Constructive criticism, builds a better sense of judgement
• Just don't let someone else's better sense of judgement
•Interfere with the criticism, that's your constructively judging

You can always read in-between the Devilish lies
•By telling people the God honest truth
• But you can never read in-between the God honest truth
•By always telling people a bunch of Devilish lies

Never believe the lies told by Devilish people
• Because those stories, have the potential and the power
• To twist and manipulate, the God honest truth

•Don't Quote Me

Who would you want by your side in times of need
- People who sit at the table with you, when it's time to eat
- Or people who put food on the table, when you're hungry

When life throws you a bone and your house broken relationship
- Gets buried by the animal behavior, of people you hang around
- Do yourself a favor and get a trained pet

Compliment a person and they'll remember it
Throughout the rest of their day
- Award a person for their outstanding goals and achievements
- And they'll remember it, throughout the rest of their life

•Don't Quote Me

We all need that someone, to help bring out the best in us
- •But when you help bring out the best in someone else
  - • That's one of the best things in life you can do

When aiming and firing an attack at someone mentally
- • With a gun temper, that's triggered by acts of violence
- •You assassinate their character, shoot down their self-esteem
  - •And kill their whole mental existence

Success, will bring new friends out and keep haters in your face
- • So, when removing the wool from over your eyes
  - • Watch how them haters and new friends
    all of sudden switch place

•INTERPET

THURSDAY

•Don't Quote Me

*E*ver lost someone in your family, that you didn't know
 • Then you realized that you knew them very well
  • Because family is all you know

*Y*ou ever got stabbed in the back, by someone you trust
• If so, it might be because whenever wealth was in front of you
 • You trusted that person, to stand right behind you

*W*atch those friends who stand next you
But decided to stop talking to you
• Because that same friend, who's now standing in front of you
 •Will be the same friend talking about you, behind your back

•Don't Quote Me

Always strive to make a winning impression
•That way champions who are winning
•Will always strive to impress you, by continuing to win

Life is like a dream
• The good ones never last long enough
• And the bad ones, wakes you right on up

In life, a lot of people will rob steal and kill
• To get what they want, in order to make ends meet
• While some people will just make ends meet
and get exactly what they want

•Don't Quote Me

We all will suffer once or twice in life
•Just don't get to the end of life, before you finally realize
•That it was the suffering, that brought your life to an end

Don't judge people by the color of their skin
•Judge them by the sins, they continue to commit
•To people of all colors, who continue getting wrongfully judged

Let the wrong people continue coaching your career
•And your flight to success in life
•Will always be one ticket away, from becoming first class

•Don't Quote Me

A *promise in life should forever be a promise*
•*Unless you made the decision, to drop your honest obligation*
•*And then all of a sudden, your sincere oath got broken*

N*ever underestimate the power of words*
•*Especially when they continue getting those around you inspired*
•*When using strong adjectives, effective nouns and influential verbs*

Y*ou're better off biting your tongue*
•*Then telling a painful lie*
•*To someone, who's already been hurt by the truth*

•Don't Quote Me

*L*et the wounds you've suffered with in the Past
•Remind you, of what to avoid in the Present
•So, those scars will continue to heal into the Future

*R*espect those who put food on the less fortunate tables
•And not those, who unfortunately only show up
when it's time to eat

*I*n this athletic sport on earth, that we call life
•One should have a healthy, professional career move
•One that's positive and constructive, with life-long benefits

•TRANSLATE

FRIDAY

•Don't Quote Me

*T*ry to avoid running around with War today
 •When you're out and about in the world
  •Because it might be the reason Peace,
   Walked away from you yesterday

*D*on't ever let depressed people, keep you from pressing on
And if it's their depression, that keeps you around these people
 •Try pressing on throughout their entire depression

*H*elp out those less fortunate than you today
 •Because blessings come in disguises, worn by those same people
  •Who unfortunately, you might have neglected just yesterday

•Don't Quote Me

While your career is in the driver's seat
•Acknowledge those who are influenced by you
•Stuck in traffic, still struggling in the street

If you wake up and you can feel inspiration touching your gut
•You're not feeding your creative imaginations full potential
•And your desire for motivation, hasn't quite yet eaten enough

You'll never starve
With hungry, ambitious driven people around you
•Who has an appetite for serving, nourishing food for thought
•And pours glasses of self-esteem
filled with uplifting encouragement

•Don't Quote Me

We all know some people with trust issues
- •Maybe it's because, every time
- •They look at themselves In the mirror
- •They have an issue with trusting who they are seeing

You could give any child on earth a gun and eventually
- •They will grow up raising bullets
- •But if you give a bullet, to any gun on earth
- •A lot of children won't be fortunate enough to grow up

If all your life, you've been violently fighting personal Battles
- •And struggling with yourself, unable to salvage some Peace
- •Then check home first, because that's where the War might have started

•Don't Quote Me

By tuning into negative channels from your past
•You'll never be able to watch and enjoy the benefits
•While controlling future episodes, of your present life

Discouraged because everything is going wrong in life
•Try learning from those who are doing the right thing in life
•By correcting those mistakes, they made in life

Opinions are personal views, thoughts and ideas
•So, when making an opinion with your own personal judgement
•Make sure your personal views, thoughts and ideas
are based on actual facts

PARAPHRASE

SATURDAY

•Don't Quote Me

If you continue getting inspired, by what people are saying
•*But never learn nothing, by the examples*
They expose in front of you
•*Then continue watching what they say*

Some people will chew an arm and a leg off of you
•*Even though you unselfishly, continue to help them out in life*
•*And that's why they have no problem*
biting the hand that's feeding them

If you hang around nine role models
•*Then you are bound to become the tenth one*
•*Who can inspire and motivate people*
hanging around your modeled role

•Don't Quote Me

Whenever the heart is filled and concerned with doubt
•It generates a conviction of worry and fear within people
  •All escalating from what they don't understand

Don't continue getting yourself harmed and disrespected
•By turning the other cheek and letting the evil of others prevail
•Because it's not the righteousness in you, that should fight back
  •But basically, it's your godly right never to fail

In the struggle, any conversation about becoming successful
  •Is built on hunger, but when you're already successful
   •There is no such thing as a struggling conversation
    •Because the appetite for success, is already gone

•Don't Quote Me

Don't ever look at yourself in the mirror
•Get discouraged and decide, you hate what you see
•Because the same person looking back at you, from the mirror
•Is God's reflection of what he created and inspired you to be

It's not about trust, when a position of power is involved
•It's about believing in that person, who's holding that position
•Because when you believe in that person and not the position
•You trust that this person, will always do the right thing

Why not shoot scholar rounds of ammunition, from your mind
•That teaches thoughts and gives A+ grades to unschooled ideas
• Why not heal suffering feelings wounded by personal battles
• To help you graduate from struggling classrooms
right next to your homeroom fears

•Don't Quote Me

*N*ever think hitting rock bottom, is the end to your life

•When basically, It's just the beginning of a new struggle

•To getting back to the highest time, place and event

• In your life from when you first fell

*W*hat's the use of patients and endurance

•If you aren't willing to go through the trials and tribulations

•That's motivated by a divine purpose

•To help you reach those heavenly goals

*V*iolence was never the key

•It's just another door, that lets you enter another room

•To help you house more and more empty violence

REPEAT

SUNDAY

•Don't Quote Me

(Blank Verse)

Don't write poetry

Into a glass of designed feelings and emotions-

Distinctively tailored by thoughts and ideas

That give styles to literature

-Po' et

•**Don't Quote Me**

(Meaning)

PO·EM /ˈpōəm, pōm/ (Noun)
•A *composition written in metrical forming rhythmical lines*

Glass Tongue

(End Rhyme)

•Tell me what you would do
If your tongue, was made up of glass

Would you try and avoid, all crystal-clear conversations
That could see right through your fractured past

By covering your face with both hands
So, the people talking to you can avoid the out-spoken blast

Or would you keep quiet and just listen
To protect all of your delicate words from shattering

By carefully pouring out, thirst-quenching thoughts and ideas
Of what your observation of views, is still constantly imagining

(Glass Tongue)

And when a full substance of news
Gives an appetite that can't be consumed
Your dialog for hunger kicks-in
Leaving malnourished discussions in the room

So, tell me what you would do
If your tongue was made up of glass

Would you try and avoid, all crystal clear conversations
That could see right through your fractured past

Or would you immediately open your loudmouth
Speak softly and try your hardest not to break the silence

Hoping that your heavy lectures and substantial speeches
Will not come across as too powerful, furious and violent

(Glass Tongue)

Or would you discipline and imprison,
All the criminal whispers in the air
To make sure all the discussions and made-up gossip
That's being told about you, is being told truthfully and fair

And when you drop an intimidating paragraph
Purposely on the ground Fearful sentences get picked-up
By scared people needing to read in-between the lines

So, you polish old remarks and clean up tarnished observations
To prove to people listening
They can get a proper understanding about your shine

Or would you rather shape, mold and perfect your verbal craft
So that the conjunctions, prepositions
And interjections within discussions either gets honored
By applause, or criticized and thrown in the trash

(Glass Tongue)

And with your brain acting as the steering the wheel
Your mind helps avoid all major accidents, when you speak
Your mentality becomes the passenger
While you sit confident in the driver's seat

On the road your words will guide you
Not to talk off course and crash
Especially when your pronunciation, switch lanes
On articulated highways and your mouth doesn't get exhausted
By your tongue moving too fast

You step on the speech pedal and let what you say
Control the steering wheel
And when the narratives in the storylines
Intelligently take charge, you start thinking real slick
Like when the oil in your ideas starts to spill

(Glass Tongue)

You become addicted to air bagging
Everything your thoughts decide to think
And with logic you'll never miss spell, what you write down
Even when closing your eyes to exchange verses, gossip and blink

So, tell me what you would do
If your tongue was made up of glass

Would you try and avoid, all crystal clear conversations
That could see right through your fractured past

Or would you use your vocabulary as a sword
To chop down peoples fabricated lies

While staring in the faces, of dirty discussions and arguments
You start having questions of doubt
By the foul look and mistrust in people's eyes

(Glass Tongue)

Hoping it doesn't impair your expressions every time
A one on one begin to arise, forcing you to bite your tongue
When you know the person you're talking to, has a vulgar mouth
And curses at you through a mask on their face in disguise

So, you speak with authority
And hope the sound in your voice, infiltrate the mass
While trying your hardest, to get people to listen and recognize
The real reason your tongue was made up of Glass...

- Glass Tongue

•Don't Quote Me

(Blank Verse)

*G*uns have a mind of their own

It's the shooters, who's not thinking-

Pulling no conscious index fingers

On stupid triggers, that's brainless-

Leaving dummy bullets, to do all the teaching...

•Don't Quote Me

(Informal Acronym)

GHET•TO /ˈɡedō/ noun

•*Geniuses Heaven Entrepreneurs Together Tackling Oppression*

•Don't Quote Me

(End of Quote)

copyright©2020

Copyright©2020

www.ingramcontent.com/pod-product-compliance
Lightning Source LLC
Chambersburg PA
CBHW050447010526
44118CB00013B/1721